THE STORY OF HERCULES

By Ingrid Griffin

Gareth Stevens
PUBLISHING

Please visit our website, www.garethstevens.com. For a free color catalog of all our high-quality books, call toll free 1-800-542-2595 or fax 1-877-542-2596.

J292.13
Griffin

Library of Congress Cataloging-in-Publication Data

Griffin, Ingrid, author.
The story of Hercules / Ingrid Griffin.
     pages cm. — (Stories in the stars)
Includes bibliographical references and index.
ISBN 978-1-4824-2669-4 (pbk.)
ISBN 978-1-4824-2670-0 (6 pack)
ISBN 978-1-4824-2671-7 (library binding)
1. Heracles (Greek mythological character)—Juvenile literature. 2. Hercules (Roman mythological character)—Juvenile literature. 3. Mythology, Greek—Juvenile literature. 4. Constellations—Folklore—Juvenile literature. 5. Hercules (Constellation)—Folklore—Juvenile literature. I. Title.
BL820.H5G75 2016
292.1'3—dc23
                            2014049057

Published in 2016 by
Gareth Stevens Publishing
111 East 14th Street, Suite 349
New York, NY 10003

Designer: Nicholas Domiano
Editor: Therese Shea

Photo credits: Cover, pp. 1, 21 (Hercules) Sergey Mikhaylov/Shutterstock.com; cover, p. 1 (stars) nienora/Shutterstock.com; p. 5 Yganko/Shutterstock.com; pp. 7, 11, 19 Print Collector/Hulton Archive/Getty Images; p. 9 Raphael GAILLARDE/Gamma-Rapho/Getty Images; p. 13 PHAS/Universal Images Group/Getty Images; pp. 15, 17 Heritage Images/ Hulton Fine Art Collection/Getty Images.

Printed in the United States of America

CPSIA compliance information: Batch #CS15GS: For further information contact Gareth Stevens, New York, New York at 1-800-542-2595.

CONTENTS

Boldface words appear in the glossary.

Hero in the Sky

A constellation is a group of stars that forms a shape. Some constellations look a bit like people. The constellation Hercules (HUHR-kyuh-leez) was named for a famous hero from **myths**. Look at this constellation with lines connecting its stars on the next page.

4

A Greek scientist named the constellation more than 2,000 years ago. Greek myths told about a hero named Heracles (HEHR-uh-kleez). The scientist thought the stars looked like Heracles **kneeling**. The Romans later called the same hero Hercules in their myths.

Meet Hercules

In Roman myths, Hercules was the son of the king of the gods, Jupiter. Jupiter's wife Juno hated Hercules. She put snakes in his crib to kill him. However, baby Hercules was already superstrong and killed the snakes!

Later, Juno made Hercules go **insane**. He killed his family. Hercules was very unhappy. He asked an **oracle** what he should do. The oracle told him to go to King Eurystheus (yuh-RIHS-thee-uhs). He would give Hercules hard jobs to do.

Juno

The Twelve Labors

King Eurystheus hated Hercules, just like Juno did. He gave Hercules 12 impossible jobs, or labors. The king didn't think Hercules could do them. The first job was to kill the terrible Nemean (NEE-mee-uhn) lion. Hercules killed the man-eating lion with his bare hands!

13

Hercules next killed a creature with 12 heads, the Hydra. He caught a deer with golden horns and a dangerous wild pig. He cleaned some dirty **stables** by moving the paths of rivers! Then, he killed deadly birds that ate people.

15

Next, Hercules caught a magic bull and man-eating horses. He took the belt of an Amazon queen and a giant's cattle. Hercules then stole golden apples guarded by a dragon. Some think the constellation shows Hercules standing on the dragon's head!

17

In the final labor of Hercules, he went to the **underworld** to bring back the mean three-headed dog called Cerberus (SUHR-buh-ruhs). He **wrestled** the dog and took it to King Eurystheus. Finally, Hercules was done with his labors.

Look Up!

Hercules had even more **adventures** in his life. When he was old, his father Jupiter placed him in the sky for all to see. On the next clear night, try to find the hero Hercules's constellation for yourself!

τ
φ
π
θ
ρ
π
ζ
ε
ο
μ
λ
δ
β
ν
α

21

GLOSSARY

adventure: an exciting or dangerous event

insane: having a serious illness of the mind

kneel: to place the body so that one or both knees are on the ground

myth: a story that was told by an ancient people to explain something

oracle: in ancient Greece, a person through whom a god was believed to speak

stable: a building in which horses are kept

underworld: a place where dead people go in myths

wrestle: to fight by gripping, holding, and pushing rather than hitting

FOR MORE INFORMATION

BOOKS

Denton, Shannon Eric. *Hercules.* Edina, MN: Magic Wagon, 2008.

Whiting, Jim. *Hercules.* Hockessin, DE: Mitchell Lane Publishers, 2008.

York, M. J. *The Constellation Hercules: The Story of the Hero.* Mankato, MN: Child's World, 2013.

WEBSITES

Herakles
www.historyforkids.org/learn/greeks/religion/myths/herakles.htm
Find out more about the myth of this famous hero.

Hercules Constellation
www.constellation-guide.com/constellation-list/hercules-constellation/
Read about Hercules and the stars in his constellation.

INDEX